A Preacher's Guide

The Psalms

ISBN 978-1-7327894-0-1

The New Life Church Preacher's Guide Series intends to strengthen and equip the work of preachers and teachers who labor faithfully in the ministry of God's Word.

Each guide is developed by members of New Life Church's teaching team and can be used as an aid to preaching, teaching, or small group study.

It is our hope that you and your team would be enriched by what you find here. Feel free to reach out to us with comments, suggestions, or questions (AArndt@newlifechurch.org).

Grace to you,

The New Life Church Teaching Team

Contents

Prepared By

Andrew Arndt

With Glenn Packiam, Daniel Grothe, and Jason R. Jackson

Preface

A brief note on this guide:

In general, the practice of our New Life Church Preacher's Guide Series is to comment on each chapter or section of the book of the Bible in question, in preparation first and foremost for our own sermon delivery.

As there are 150 Psalms, we felt an obvious need as we approached our sermon series in the Spring of 2018 to limit ourselves, choosing a handful of the Psalms members of our team had found most meaningful in the course of their own personal walks with the Lord.

This guide, therefore, is a reflection on those Psalms.

Our hope is that even if the specific Psalm(s) you are planning to preach or teach is not contained in this guide, at the very least, by reading it, you will have learned something of the method by and spirit in which we interpreted and applied the contents of the Psalter. In so doing, we trust your own ministry of the Word will have been greatly strengthened.

x

Introduction

Why do we love the Psalms so? One could drop into the Psalter almost at random to illustrate the point I would like to make, but consider for a moment one of our most beloved, Psalm 63:

> *You, God, are my God,*
> *earnestly I seek you;*
> *I thirst for you,*
> *my whole being longs for you,*
> *in a dry and parched land*
> *where there is no water...* (v.1)

It is hard to read such words and retain any semblance of objectivity. More or less immediately, a transition begins to occur in *how* we are engaging the text. We move from being detached observers to finding ourselves caught up, involved, even *implicated* in the poetry. The words on the page mysteriously and perhaps even without our noticing it become *ours*.

> *On my bed I remember you;*
> *I think of you through the watches of the night.*
> *Because you are my help,*
> *I sing in the shadow of your wings.*
> *I cling to you;*
> *your right hand upholds me...* (vv. 6-8).

Before we know it, we find ourselves claiming the words of the Psalmist as *our own* words, as devastatingly accurate statements on the condition of *our own* souls, as cries emerging from the depths of *our own* lives. *We* are the thirsty ones. *We* are the ones who long for God as in a dry and weary land. *We* are the ones who remember God on our beds, whose hearts search for him during the long watches of dark and desolate nights. *We* are the ones clinging to him with all our might, finding therein our lives mysteriously upheld by his righteous right hand.

And so we sit, early in the morning or late at night or during a break in our busy day, with the text of Scripture on our laps, walking the pattern of spiritual devotion that the Psalmist many centuries earlier laid out for us by taking these ancient-yet-living words on our lips. In so doing, deep reservoirs of emotion open up in us. Tears fall. Joy surges. Hope returns. And even more: When our time of devotion is concluded we discover that the words of the Psalmist are, entirely on their own (so it seems), burrowing into our souls, creating new patterns of thought and feeling and action. Before long, the deep music of our days and weeks and months and years goes something like: *You God, are my God, earnestly I seek you…*

This is the power of the Psalter. It is one of the important reasons it is part of our canon. It *speaks* to us where we are but refuses to *leave* us where we are. The Psalms, we may say, *convert* us precisely by *involving* us—messy, complex, altogether unfinished, and full of contradictions—in the great cogent sweep of God's redemptive work. It does this by putting words on our lips and inviting us to make them ours. John Goldingay notes that "the Bible assumes that we do not know instinctively how to talk with God but rather need some help with knowing how to do so."[1] The Psalms are instruction. It's no wonder that many have theorized that the five books of the Psalter are intended to correspond symbolically to the five books of the Pentateuch. *When we come to the Psalms, we are entering the school of prayer.* Martin Luther commented that the Psalms were given to us in order to help us "adapt and adjust our minds and feelings so that they are in accord with the sense of the Psalms,"[2] which for Luther were a picture into the will of God for his people.

We are not born into this world instinctively knowing what is available to us in covenant relationship with God. But the Psalms can teach us; they "make it possible to say things that are otherwise unsayable...they have the capacity to free us to talk about things we cannot talk about anywhere else."[3] The Book of Psalms dignifies our lives by converting our imaginations to a God-enriched, covenant-shaped world, fraught with challenge and yet shot through everywhere with energetic hope. *"My God, my God, why have you forsaken me...?"* finds its completion in *"They will proclaim his righteousness, declaring to a people yet unborn: He has done it!"* (Psalm 22). The ebb and flow of desolation and exultation, of lament and praise, is the texture of the Psalms, even as it is the texture of our very lives. When we pray the Psalms, we find the music of our little peaks and valleys caught up in the great *fugue* of God's historical, redemptive work.

---

1   John Goldingay. Psalms. (Baker Commentary on the Old Testament. Baker Academic, 2008.) Vol. 1, Page 22.

2   Luther, Selected Psalms, 3:310 as quoted in Goldingay, p. 22.

3   Goldingay, pp. 22-23.

The philosopher Charles Taylor has noted that the secular age in which we live is what he calls a "cross-pressured" age.[4] The collapse of the old way of looking at the world has created a profound disenchantment. Modern people no longer automatically see the world as lit up with the incandescent splendor of divine light. "God" or "the gods" are not operative factors in our thinking. And yet, he says, we are *haunted*—if not by the belief then certainly by the *longing* that there must be "more." But many do not know where to turn to find that "more."

That is one pressure. The other pressure, according to Taylor, is that belief is *contested*. To subscribe to the sort of world laid out for us in the Scriptures is no easy task. The old cultural supports for religious faith in Western civilization have waned. Saying "We believe" or "I believe" will cost you something, and the road will be continually fraught with challenge. Neither sainthood nor cynicism in our modern age are entirely without peril.

And that is precisely what makes the Book of Psalms a great friend to the preacher and pastor. They speak to that cross-pressured situation with profound eloquence. To the "haunted cynic," the Psalmist says: "*Go ahead. Try it. Take the words of Psalm 19 on your lips and see what happens. What if it were true? What if the heavens were telling the glory of God? What if indeed the universe is haunted? What then will happen to your cozy life?*" Wonder and mystery suddenly begin to impinge. Cracks in the old frame of reference become visible. Light from another world shines through. And to the believer who finds their faith contested on

---

4   Charles Taylor, *A Secular Age* (Harvard University Press, 2007), as summarized by James K. A. Smith in *How (Not) To Be Secular: Reading Charles Taylor* (Eerdmans, 2014).

every front, the Psalmist sidles up alongside them and says: *"Welcome to the Story. You are part of a long and proud line of folks who have had to bite and scrape and claw for their faith every step of the way. You are not alone...many have gone before you; many are with you even now."*

And just then, we find a new dimension of the Psalter's power opening to us. *For the Book of Psalms is, before it is anything else, the Church's book.* Helpful as the poetry of St. John of the Cross may be, moving as the music of Rachmaninov may be, they are still the expressions of single individuals giving voice to hope and longing and devotion. The Psalms are different. Gathered up by the Church as "canon," the Psalms introduce us to a *people* whose lives, both in their peaks and their valleys, are caught up in covenant devotion. The Psalms, whether we are reading them on our own or doing so in the company of other faithful followers, bring us into the *congregation* shaped by the mighty deeds of God: Father, Son, and Holy Spirit. That is, *the subject* of the Psalms, the one who is praying them, is always the Church, and we as members of it. The Psalms remind us that *the Faith is not "discovered" but "given" to us by others, and we are never alone.* We don't have the luxury of imagining ourselves as isolated individuals when we pray the Psalms, for the Psalms unite us with the whole People of God, visible and invisible, past and future and present, who are themselves gathered up by the power of the Holy Spirit to God the Father in the person of Jesus Christ. The Psalms are the single, united prayer of the Body of Christ to the Triune God. Whenever and wherever we pray them, *we are not alone.*

And with that insight, one further secret of the Psalms is unlocked. The Church is called "The Body of Christ" because she has been *incorporated* into Christ. Christ himself is both her unifying and animating principle. Dietrich Bonhoeffer said it like no one else could:

> *A psalm that we cannot utter as a prayer, that makes us falter and horrifies us, is a hint to us that here Someone else is praying, not we; that the One who is here protesting his innocence, who is invoking God's judgment, who has come to such infinite depths of suffering, is none other than Jesus Christ himself. He it is who is praying here, and not only here but in the whole Psalter...The Man Jesus Christ, to whom no affliction, no ill, no suffering is alien, and who yet was the wholly innocent and righteous one, is praying in the Psalter through the mouth of his Church. The Psalter is the prayer book of Jesus Christ in the truest sense of the word. He prayed the Psalter and now it has become his prayer for all time...Jesus Christ prays the Psalter in his congregation...[it] is the vicarious prayer of Christ for his Church. Now that Christ is with the Father, the new humanity of Christ, the Body of Christ on earth, continues to pray his prayer to the end of time."[5]*

Bonhoeffer is saying what the Church has always, in some form or fashion, held: No engagement with the Psalter can be called Christian that does not recognize in its staggeringly beautiful cadence the presence and voice of the utterly unique and representative human, Jesus Christ, God who has come to us in flesh, taking our deepest hopes and fears and longings up into his infinite life. Jesus, if we have eyes to see him, is *there*. Praying over us. Praying for us. Weeping with us. In the hopes and joys of the Psalms, in their desperate pleas and urgent

---

5   Dietrich Bonhoeffer. *Life Together* (Harper and Row, 1954), pp 45-46.

petitions, Christ is there, leading us, together, into the future that awaits us as children of the Father—Jesus' Father, and now, by faith, ours as well. *God*, we may say, *prays to God* in the Psalter, in and with and through us: *"You, God, are my God; earnestly I seek you..."* When we do not know what to pray, Jesus is right there, in the pages of the Psalter, carrying us home. This is their power.

Suggestions for Preaching the Psalms

Accordingly, here are a few things to keep in mind when you preach the Psalms

Let the poetry of the Psalms loose on the congregation. Part of what makes the Psalms compelling is the *way* in which they communicate. The Psalms are not prose. They are poetry. Even more, they are *song*. They do not speak quite the way that a parable or a long didactic section of an epistle speak. Metaphor, suggestion, imagery: this is the stock-in-trade of the Psalms. As you prepare, look at several different translations. Watch how they handle each word and turn of phrase. Feel the power of the images in your time of personal devotion, and let that felt power be a source of prophetic inspiration for you, and, in turn, for the congregation. When you preach your psalm, you might consider having the congregation read it out loud along with you. Let them *feel* it. Help them make its urgent pleas and courageous doxologies *theirs*.

Let the humanity of the Psalms teach. As Goldingay has noted, the Psalms help us "say the unsayable." I am not sure that we would feel justified in accusing God of forsaking us or asking him to strike down our enemies if the Psalms had not said, *"Go ahead. Try it. We went there before you."* But so it is. The Psalms by their very nature invite us into a certain "complexifying" of our humanity that we would not have had otherwise. They invite us to leave behind flat, wooden, simplistic ways of understanding ourselves in relationship to God, calling us into the living dynamism of actual covenant relationship. The Psalms say to us, *"Your anger, your doubt, your frustration, your failure, your dread… it all belongs here, before the face of the God who made you and loves you."*

Remember the greater Story that the Psalms emerge from and point to. The Psalms are a window into the genuinely *human* side of the Story of Scripture. As such, each is powerful, and each is also limited. When the Psalmist cries out, "Break the teeth in their mouths, O God!" (Ps 58:6), we are getting a glimpse into what it feels like to be violated by the wicked. The cry for vengeance is a profound testimony to the Scriptures' uniform claim that our God is a God who loves righteousness and hates wickedness, and will one day right all wrongs. It is *descriptively* powerful. But "Break the teeth in their mouths" is not a *prescription* for the faithful. The God to whom we cry out is always and can never be other than the God revealed in Jesus, who said, "Be merciful, just as your Father is merciful" (Luke 6:36). Likewise, "My God, my God, why have you forsaken me?" is descriptively powerful as a testimony to how we often feel. And yet, we are those who live on the far side of the Son's cry from the cross: *Eloi, eloi, lama sabachtani…* The 2nd Person of the Trinity, Christ the Lord, is God of very God who has taken all God-forsakenness into himself and overcome it. The wise preacher will preach with an awareness of the greater Story *while nevertheless acknowledging* that the human journey to embrace the high call of Jesus in all its fullness is never easy.

Let the Psalms lead your listeners to Jesus. It is not hard to do, and requires no high-flying exegetical maneuvers. The God the Psalmists prayed to and pleaded with is eternally the Father of Jesus Christ, who, as the Nicene Creed declares, "for us and for our salvation...was made man." As we have said, if those claims are true, then it is ultimately *to* Jesus (with his Father, in the power of the Spirit) that the prayers of the Psalms are addressed, and it is *by* Jesus that the prayers are uttered, and it is *with* Jesus that the Church prays them. When we, for instance, preach Psalm 1: *"Blessed is the one who does not walk in step with the wicked, or stand in the way that sinners take, or sit in the seat of mockers,"* we are invited to hear the words of Jesus: "I am the Way, and the Truth, and the Life" (John 14:6). We likewise summon our hearers to embrace him, to walk with him. The psalm becomes a powerful picture of Christian discipleship. Even more, we are invited to see in the psalm a picture of Christ himself, who delighted in the instruction of his Father, who knew that his own "way" was watched over by the Father, both into and beyond the grave, and whose faithful obedience becomes our own. Psalm 1 opens a door into the entire drama of our life with God *now*, our Jesus-devotion *now*. And in their own unique way, all the rest of the Psalms do as well.

Psalm 1

A Prayer for Living Well

This psalm seems like it was composed with the purpose of being the opening prayer for the whole prayer book that is the Psalter. It has many of the marks of "wisdom literature" particularly in its contrasts between two ways of living. Derek Kidner sees it as functioning as a "doorkeeper" for the one who wishes to be in the "assembly of the faithful" (v. 5b)[1]: *You want to join the worshipping congregation? Choose this kind of life and not the other.*

The structure of the psalm is roughly bookended by the "negatives"— warnings about the things not to do, the way not to live (v. 1), and the consequences of ignoring those warnings (vv. 4-5). This places the "positive" injunction at the very heart of the psalm. *Live like this (v. 2), and you will truly live (v. 3).* This approach has parallels in the renewal of the covenant in Deuteronomy 28 and the prophetic call in Jeremiah 17, the latter of which has an expanded version of the tree metaphor.

The heart of the psalm is a twofold call to *delight* and to *meditate* on the *instruction* or *direction* of the Lord. It has to do with *desire* and *action*, or habit. The work of God in us must be *inward* and *outward;* it changes us from the inside out, and from the outside in. It is not enough to have the

---

1   Derek Kidner, *Psalms 1-72* (InterVarsity Press, 2008): p. 63.

right motives or desires; we must cultivate the right habits and practices. In the New Testament, Paul will say the God working in us leads us both to *desire* and *do* God's will (Phil. 2:13). Kidner notes that the word for "meditate" is the same as the word used for "plot" in Psalm 2:1b, and one can see how two completely differently lives result from the two disparate objections of contemplation: Meditate on how God rules the world and you will flourish; meditate on your plans for ruling the world and you will fail[2].

The kind of flourishing that results is a kind that is unfazed by external circumstances. Goldingay notes that in a Middle Eastern climate, there are long dry seasons that come "when a fruit tree most needs water as its fruit grows to maturity,"[3] and therefore must be planted by a stream for its roots to reach. Such a tree is not at the mercy of external sources of nourishment for it has found a deeper source. So it is for the person who turns again and again to the instruction and direction of the Lord.

The final verse in the psalm is a summary with one clear pronouncement: YHWH himself is the reason the life of the faithful flourishes. This is the first mention of God in the prayer, and it comes so that we know that *God and his attentiveness is the reason for life working out.* Moreover, we learn that *faithfulness to YHWH matters.* It will produce what we think it should: a flourishing life. This conviction shapes a sense of justice rooted in God's own character of faithfulness. And it is that justice and faithfulness to which the Psalmist appeals in the prayers that follow when it seems that the wicked are prospering and the righteous are

---

2   Ibid., p. 64.

3   John Goldingay, *The Psalms*. Vol. 1, p. 84.

suffering.

Preaching Pathways

1. **Sometimes God has to turn us away from something *destructive* before he can turn us toward something *instructive* and *productive*.** What do you need to turn away from in your life? How can you turn more toward the instruction of the Lord?

2. **Is there a link between our desires and our habits?** Do we say we want to grow in the Lord but ignore developing the disciplines that will cultivate the conditions for such growth?

3. **What do we believe about God's sense of justice?** Does faithfulness to God really lead to flourishing? This tension can be explored in order to root people in God's character and to orient them toward an ultimate (or eschatological) justice—which is, of course, part of God's judgment.

4. **God's attentiveness to our life is the reason for its flourishing.** If his Word is the water, his face is the sunshine. Where do we need to believe that God is smiling on us, even in our small and seemingly insignificant faithfulness to him?

Prayer from *Common Worship*

Christ, our Wisdom, give us delight in your law, that we bear fruits of patience and peace in the kingdom of the righteous, for your mercy's sake. Amen.

Psalm 2

Who Is in Charge?

"Blessed is the one who…" begins Psalm 1. *"Blessed are all who…"* ends Psalm 2. The Hebrew word used for "blessed" in each instance is the same: *ashre*—happy, blessed, fortunate. We might say that *ashre* is a word used to answer the question: "Who is *well off? Who is living the good life?"* Psalms 1 and 2 together paint a complementary picture of the good life. Whereas in Psalm 1 the "blessed" person is the one who delights in Yahweh's instruction; in Psalm 2 the "blessed" person is the one who recognizes Yahweh's authentic rule as the Israelite King and submits himself/herself willingly to Yahweh. The focal point of each psalm may be different, but the *ethos* is undeniably the same: Yahweh's will and ways are the backbone and deep texture of the universe; the wise person will behave accordingly.

Psalm 2 clearly belongs in the category of a "royal psalm," which, along with a handful of others, celebrates the rule of Yahweh through the agency of the Israelite King, who in verse 2 is called the *mashiach* ("anointed"; this Hebrew word is where we get the word "Messiah") and in verses 7 and 12 is called Yahweh's "son." It is easy to see how the early church seized upon this and similar psalms as descriptions of the identity and vocation of Jesus Christ (Messiah): He is the Anointed Son of God who fills up in his own person what the Israelite kings of old could never really do or be. The kings of the earth and the rulers may indeed band together against him—and in point of fact, they did when Rome and Jerusalem colluded in the murder of Jesus—but the One enthroned in heaven threw his head back, laughed, and raised the great King David's "Greater Son"[1] from the dead, enthroning him at his right hand in glory, never to see decay.

The powers that be still rage to this day. The headlines tell that story on a daily basis. But rest assured: Yahweh and his Son will have their day. Seen through this lens, Psalm 2 is a powerful summons to all nations and rulers and people everywhere to bend the knee in worship of Jesus, the Lord, whose kingdom was and is and ever will be without end.

Preaching Pathways

1. **The public nature of faith**. A perennial temptation in Christianity is to reduce faith to "inwardness"—to a private, personal encounter with the Lord that has nothing to do with public life. Though faith certainly *is* personal and private, it is not a purely inward matter. The God we meet in private devotion is the Lord of all the earth, and he reigns through his Son, Jesus. One day all people everywhere will recognize this. The "blessed" life is one that recognizes it now.

2. **Faith is *allegiance* and it is focused on a *Person***. In a similar vein, another temptation of Christianity is to reduce faith to mere "belief";

---

1   From the hymn, *Hail to the Lord's Anointed* (James Montgomery, 1771-1854). The preacher may find this hymn a useful tool in his/her sermon prep.

that is, it is about the proper arrangement of cognitive religious content. This psalm mitigates powerfully against that view. Faith here is about what we might call *fealty;* that is, allegiance: Do we swear allegiance to God's King, Jesus, or do we live our lives in rebellion against heaven's rule? That is the question this psalm poses.

Prayer from *Common Worship*

Most high and holy God, lift our eyes to your Son enthroned on Calvary; and as we behold his meekness, shatter our earthly pride; for he is the Lord for ever and ever. Amen.

Psalm 22

A Prayer of Lament and Hope

Psalm 22 is one of the most well-known psalms in the prayer book, though not necessarily because it is well-loved but because of its association with Jesus. There is no doubt that this psalm figures prominently in the accounts of the death and resurrection of Christ, but it cannot be viewed simply as "prophecy." **It is first a portrait of how one can hold two things in tension: the *experience of suffering* and the *confidence of redemption*.**

Lament **and** *hope* **come together in this psalm.** Verses 1-20 form the first half, while verses 22-31 form the second; verse 21 serves as the hinge. Goldingay outlines three types of experiences of suffering that the psalm names. The first is the experience of being overwhelmed. The second is the experience of persecution at the hands of enemies. The third is the experience of God's absence. Goldingay also identifies four things that the psalm invites us to do in order to ground our hope[1]. First, we can remind God and ourselves of his past acts of deliverance. Secondly, we can remind God and ourselves of God's involvement in our own lives. Thirdly, we can move from reminders to petitions, urging God to change his perceived course of action and to be near and to act on our behalf. Finally, we can begin to believe that God will respond.

---

1   Goldingay, Vol. 1, p. 340.

But this psalm is not just about *our* experience of suffering and our attempt to hang on to hope. Just as we cannot read this psalm simply as a prophecy about Jesus, neither can we read it simply as a portrait of how to hold lament and hope together. Because of the way the New Testament uses this psalm to illuminate the vocation of Jesus as the suffering servant of God, we have to look closely at this psalm in the light of Christ. There are four key resonances. First, the soldiers divide Jesus' clothes (Mark 15:24 and Psalm 22:18); secondly, passersby mock and taunt him (Mark 15:29 and Psalm 22:7-8); thirdly, Christ himself says the opening words of the psalm on the cross (Mark 15:34 and Psalm 22:1); finally, the book of Hebrews places the vow to praise as words of Jesus (Hebrews 2:12 and Psalm 22:22).

What are we to make of this? How do we hold together the resonance with human experience in general and the parallels in the death and resurrection of Jesus in particular? *The key is in understanding Jesus' life, death, and resurrection as the fulfillment of Israel's vocation—which was in itself a representative of the human condition.* If Psalm 22 is meant to depict the contours of Israel's suffering and redemption, then in Jesus the story comes together in its fullest form. Jesus suffers as the True *and* Innocent Israel, faithful to YHWH to the very end (which Israel was not) and experiences the ultimate redemption (for which Israel through her prophets had hoped): *resurrection.* So, we might say that the psalm *prefigures* Jesus (rather than "predicts") precisely because Jesus *reconfigures* the Israel story by summing it up in himself.

But there's more. In summing up the Israel story, Jesus is also taking on the human story. He is, as Matthew's gospel shows, the True Israel; but he is also, as Luke's gospel shows, the True Human. And here's why that's good news: **there is no suffering, no pain, no despair, no distance from God, no alienation or dislocation that we experience that Jesus does not also know.** He has been there. Literally. And God the Father brought him out on the other side singing. And so it will be for us. Put your hope in this crucified and risen Savior. *Jesus is the place where lament and hope truly meet.*

Preaching Pathways

Lament is a form of praise precisely because it is directed to God.
By taking our lament to God, we are confessing that he is the highest authority in the universe, the Sovereign over all creation. Furthermore, by expressing lament to God, we are demonstrating our faith that he cares and that he keeps his covenant. Every lament in the psalms is rooted in the knowledge that God has made a covenant with Israel. Thus they—and we who are in Christ—appeal to God based on his promise and on his character of faithfulness.

Because Jesus took on the suffering of the world, we know that in our suffering we are not alone. Even in our own feelings of godforsakenness, we can know that Jesus has been there. Indeed, he *is* here.

We do not grieve as those who have no hope. As the Psalmist holds grief and hope together, so must the Christian. But our reason for hope is on even firmer ground. If Christ is the ultimate sufferer—the One suffered the worst fate in all of history (the Son of God crucified!)—and was raised to life by the Father, then for all who are in Christ, resurrection is coming. Because Psalm 22 comes to its fulfillment in Jesus, in his death and resurrection, we know that the worst day will not be the last day. Death will not have the final word. Forsakenness may be how we feel, but one day we will sing again.

Prayer from *Common Worship*

Restless with grief and fear, the abandoned turn to you: in every hour of trial, good Lord, deliver us, O God most holy, God most strong, whose wisdom is the cross of Christ. Amen.

Psalm 23

A Prayer to the Good Shepherd

What more can be said that has not already been said about this the most well-known and well-loved psalm of all? There is not enough space to summarize the wealth of preaching and commentating on this psalm throughout the church's history. It is worth noting just a few key things. First, Kidner notes that the metaphor of "shepherd" is the "most comprehensive and intimate metaphor yet encountered in the Psalms."[1] This is because a shepherd lives with his flock and is everything to them: "guide, physician, and protector". Moreover, the image of a shepherd is what Israel's prophets used to define the calling of Israel's kings. In Ezekiel 34, God declares that he is against Israel's shepherds because of the way they exploit and oppress the sheep instead of tending to and caring for them. They use force to rule, and as a result the sheep are scattered. God then vows to come and be the Shepherd of Israel for himself. This then is fulfilled in Jesus' declaration in John 10 that he himself is the Good Shepherd—YHWH came at last to care for his people and bring justice and peace. So, the 23rd Psalm comes to its sharpest focus in Jesus. He is the one who will provide for them, who will lead them, who will restore them, who will walk with them in the darkest valleys and comfort them; he is the one who will prepare a table for them before their enemies, who will anoint them, and who will lead them to

---

1   Derek Kidner, *Psalms 1-72* (InterVarsity Press, 2008): p. 127.

dwell with God forever.

But the 23rd Psalm comes alive in the Jesus story in another way, a much darker way. Jesus experiences the opposite of everything the Psalmist prays for. Instead of green pastures, Jesus said he had no place to lay his head; instead of quiet waters, Jesus walked on stormy seas; instead of walking through the valley of the shadow of death, Jesus walked up the hill of death—Golgotha itself. Instead of a table *before* his enemies, Jesus supped *with* his enemies, the one who proceeded to betray him. His cup ran over, but it was a not a cup of blessing but one of judgment and wrath (cf. Isaiah 51:17, 22), which he asked to pass from him, but instead drank it to the dregs. But—and here is where the words of the Psalmist come true in the end—goodness and mercy *did* follow Jesus. The Father raised him up in vindication, and he does indeed dwell in the house of God forever, seated at the right hand of the Father.

Put these two things together. Jesus is both the Good Shepherd and the sheep who suffered to the uttermost. This is the reason Psalm 23 is true for us; this is how we know that this prayer—for provision, protection, guidance, and more—will be answered in the end. Jesus is the Good Shepherd who laid down his life for his sheep. Thanks be to God!

Preaching Pathways

1. **Where do you need God's provision or protection or guidance?** You can know that God has put himself on the line: He himself has come

to dwell with you, to care for you, to shepherd you.

2. **Where do you feel like you are carrying too much weight?** Imagine David as the king, feeling the weight of leading Israel, wondering who would lead *him*. This prayer is a reminder that for all the responsibilities that we carry, it is the Lord who is carrying us.

3. **Is this a prayer that feels difficult to pray?** Know that Jesus experienced the opposite of this psalm so that it would be true for us ultimately, in the end. And even now, he is with us through the valley. And his goodness and mercy are chasing us down. They will catch us.

Prayer from *Common Worship*

O God, our sovereign and shepherd, who brought again your Son Jesus Christ from the valley of death, comfort us with your protecting presence and your angels of goodness and love, that we may also come home and dwell with him in your house forever. Amen.

Psalm 24

Who is The King of Glory?

Claus Westermann calls Psalm 24 a "liturgical psalm,"[1] and for good reason: The psalm clearly envisions a group of the faithful heading up to the Temple for worship, having prepared themselves beforehand. The psalm begins with a straightforward announcement: *"The earth is the Lord's and everything in it!"* As Abraham Kuyper once said, "There is not a square inch in the whole domain of our human existence over which Christ, who is Sovereign over all, does not cry, 'Mine!'"[2] This psalm is a powerful liturgical celebration of that claim. The question of verse 3 rings out: *"Who may ascend the hill of the Lord?"* And the answer returns (Westermann argues that this would come from one of the priests presiding over worship): *"The one who has clean hands and a pure heart"* (v.4). Those who approach the holy place in *this* way, from a posture of preparedness, reverence, and holy devotion, are those who receive the *berachah,* the "blessing" of Yahweh, which in the Old Testament denotes the release of Yahweh's power for life into and over a people or situation. Worship of the God whose claim over created reality is ultimate is literally, for the Psalmist, a matter of life and death.

---

1   Claus Westermann, *The* Psalms (Augsburg Press, 1980), pp.103-104.

2   Abraham Kuyper: *A Centennial Reader*, James D. Bratt, ed. (Eerdmans, 1998), p. 488.

The psalm suddenly pivots, however, with verse 7: *"Lift up your heads, you gates; be lifted up, you ancient doors, that the King of glory may come in."* Now the focal point is no longer the worshipers who are coming into the holy place, but the King of glory who is arriving to take up, once again, his royal residence in Jerusalem. Having triumphed on the battlefield, Israel's Mighty Warrior now returns to the seat of his power, enthroned upon the praises of his people. The city is summoned to recognize the return of its victorious God. Westermann claims that the psalm is a *liturgical enactment of that enthronement.*

Preaching Pathways

1. **Who is sovereign?** The first verse of this psalm states the matter as clearly as you will find it stated in the Psalter: everything and everyone belongs to Yahweh. In the ancient world, the "seas" or the "waters" were seen in a more or less "divine" light—they were one of many creational deities perpetually at war, and rather menacing to humans. Psalm 24:1, much like Genesis 1, pictures Yahweh in *unthreatened sovereignty* over all the created order—humans and "gods" alike. No one outranks him.

2. **"Who may ascend…?"** The psalm pictures Yahweh loyalists heading up to worship, receiving his blessing. They don't trust in idols, they don't "swear" by false gods. They are not perfect by any means. But likewise, they are not living in *intentional split allegiance*. They ascend the hill to give their lives anew to their God, and he blesses them.

This is how we should approach worship.

3. **Worship is an enactment and foretaste of what will be**. When we gather for worship, we see ahead of time what one day will be made manifest to the naked eye, to *every* naked eye, and we also in so doing make it present and tangible: the universal reign of the King of Glory.

Prayer from *Common Worship*

O Lord of hosts, purify our hearts that the King of glory may come in, your Son, Jesus our Redeemer. Amen.

Psalm 40

A Psalm of Thanksgiving and Lament

Psalm 40 is divided into two sections:

1. vv. 1-10: a song of thanksgiving

2. v. 11-17: a song of lament

Movement 1: A Song of Thanksgiving

"I waited patiently" as an opening line is too precious a translation for what's going on here. Brueggemann says the infinitive absolute might be better translated, "I hope intensely for Yahweh."[1] This person has no other options, is teetering on the precipice of destruction, and in this moment acknowledges that unless YHWH steps in, all futures cease to exist. Against all odds—and here the reader of Psalm 40 is meant to think of *Egyptian captivity* and *wilderness wandering*—YHWH breaks in and "inclines to me" having "heard my cry." He "lifted me up out of the pit" and "set my feet upon a rock" (vv. 1-3). But the rescue isn't *just* personal. It's communal. "*Many* will see it and fear and put their trust in the Lord" (v. 3).

---

1   Walter Brueggemann, *The Message of the Psalms* (Fortress Press, 1985), p. 128

The rescued one sings a "new song," which is a phrase with resonances throughout the canon (Isaiah 42:10; Ps. 96:1, 98:1; Rev. 5:9). Moses and Miriam *sing* after crossing the Sea of Reeds (Ex. 15:1-18,15:21), Mary *sings* at the annunciation of salvation (Luke 1:46-55), but so do the elders and angels and four living creatures. *When one considers Yahweh's work of salvation, explanatory prose is a dead end.* All you can do is *sing*, and the song has to be "new" because of the surprising activity of God's kindness.

But the question becomes, what does YHWH want from those he has delivered? He wants fresh obedience, "an embrace of Torah which is not burden but delight."[2] We wrongly imagine freedom to be getting to do whatever we like. Not so, says the Psalmist, and Jeremiah 31:31-34 confirms it. We're free only when we delight in choosing the way that is unselfconsciously synced up with Torah, when Torah spills out of us. Verses 8-10 indicate that the rescued one also becomes the proclaiming one, shouting the good news of salvation to the ends of the earth.

Movement 2: A Song of Lament

"Wait, I thought this psalm was supposed to be a psalm of *thanksgiving*? Why now are we lamenting?" This psalm almost has a Jekyll-and-Hyde feel to it, and it feels like it moves in reverse order. "Shouldn't we start with lament and end in thanksgiving?" But the Psalmist goes in reverse order on purpose, I think, because life doesn't follow a straight-line trajectory from defeat to victory. Some days we're celebrating and

---

2   Ibid., p. 129.

thanking God for his goodness! But sometimes the very next day feels like the bottom has fallen out and we're descending back into a time of uncertainty and difficulty and despair. This psalm makes room for that reality. Life is more complex than the "All I Do Is Win" gospel would have us believe. The petition for rescue pervades this psalm (vv. 11, 13, 17) because there are so many things we need God to help us with—the prodigal child, the physical ailment, the financial destruction at hand. The lament portion of this psalm ends by anticipating rescue ("Great is Yahweh," v. 16), but it closes by asking God not to drag his feet—"Do not tarry, O my God" (v. 17).

Preaching Pathways

1. **This psalm gives the preacher permission to name the ambiguity of life and honor those going through a time of difficulty**. We'll never go wrong by giving people who are in difficulty the permission to lament.

2. **This psalm gives the preacher the opportunity to highlight what happens for those who will wait**—Rescue *will* come! Deliverance *will* come! Victory *is* the end of our story. "Those that wait upon the Lord shall renew their strength" (Isaiah 40:31).

Prayer from *Common Worship*

Free us from our sin, O God, and may our sacrifices be of praise to the glory of your Son, our Redeemer, Jesus Christ. Amen.

Psalm 42

The Prayer of a Man Sorely Tried

Scholars don't know the historical circumstances surrounding this Psalm, but from a literary standpoint, the story is clear enough: this is the prayer of a faithful man who is being sorely tried. *"As the deer pants for the streams of water, so my soul pants for you, my God"* (v. 1). "Soul" here is the Hebrew word *nephesh*, and it means something more than what English speaking people usually mean when they use the word "soul." It means something like "the totality of my being." Every part of the Psalmist here longs for God as his aching tears fall to the ground (v. 3a). And why the tears? Because he is taunted by his enemies (v. 3). Because he has somehow been separated from his friends and fellow worshipers (v. 4). Because he is surrounded by the strange and unfamiliar and deeply hostile (v. 10). And in the midst of it, perhaps most importantly, because he feels forgotten by God (v. 9).

The psalm gives us a peek into the inner turmoil of this faithful man who is being sorely tried, and to that extent it is deeply instructive. What does he do? First, arrests his self-talk and orders it to the truth of who God was and is and will be for him: *"Why, my soul, are you downcast? Why so disturbed within me? Put your hope in God, for I will yet praise him, my Savior and my God"* (vv. 5, 11). The Psalmist refuses to let despair be the last word. He utters a word of hope to himself, encouraging himself to remember God (v. 6). Secondly, he recognizes the hidden presence of

God even in the midst of his circumstance. *"By day the Lord directs his love"* (v. 8). The word used for "love" there is *hesed*—which in the Hebrew scriptures denotes God's *covenant faithfulness*. The Psalmist believed that God's covenant faithfulness to him was at work—even in this situation of deep alienation, estrangement, and suffering— to lead him back home. So let us believe.

Preaching Pathways

1. **The experience of suffering is normal.** In our "happy clappy" consumeristic Jesus culture, it is all too easy to forget that the experience of suffering, along with feelings of loneliness, abandonment, estrangement, and alienation, are *normal* parts of our faith. Sometimes circumstances beyond our control throw our little happy lives for a loop, and we wonder where God is. Other times it is the suffering that comes to us at the hands of a disobedient world that breaks up our sense of "normal." To those in that situation, Psalm 42 says, "You are not alone."

2. **Our hope in suffering.** While the Psalmist may indeed feel "downcast" with all the "waves and breakers" of life sweeping over him, threatening to drown him, he also steadfastly refuses to give up hope. His moments of hopeful self-talk in verses 5 and 11 are no idle flights of empty fancy. They are based on the abiding *hesed* of God; that is, his "word" to himself is based on God's "first word" of covenant to him. And that is what gives him hope. He has yielded his

life to the God who binds himself to his people with cords of love that will never be broken. Our hope is never our ability to pull ourselves out of circumstances. Our hope is God's goodness. In and with us, his very Name is on the line, as Psalm 23:3 puts it. And that should lift our heavy hearts.

Prayer from *Common Worship*

Come, Creator Spirit, source of life; sustain us when our hearts are heavy and our wells have run dry, for you are the Father's gift, with him who is our living water, Jesus Christ our Lord. Amen.

Psalm 46

A Prayer for Protection

Martin Luther launched the Protestant Reformation with the Ninety-Five Theses. About ten years later, he galvanized the movement with the great hymn "A Mighty Fortress Is Our God." His fight song was inspired by Psalm 46. Since that time, this psalm has become almost synonymous with Luther. Few lifelong Protestants and even fewer cradle-to-grave Lutherans can read these words without humming his tune or thinking about his plight. This speaks to the Psalter's unique capacity to speak far beyond its time.

Psalm 46 contains three stanzas separated by a "selah" but bound together by their exaltation of God's protecting presence in the earth. In the first stanza (vv. 1-3), God shelters his people in the midst of a natural disaster. The Psalmist depicts a cataclysmic earthquake toppling the mountains into the seas, and the seas tossing tidal waves back against the mountains that remain. The image hints at the undoing of creation and the return of chaos. But because God can be found in distress, God's people declare with uncanny confidence, "We will not fear" (v. 2).

In the second verse, the Lord preserves his people in the midst of international political upheaval. He does so both in and through his holy city. Though the mountains may *shake* (Hebrew: *mot*), Jerusalem will not *move* (same word: *mot*). Though kingdoms totter (again: *mot*), God stabilizes the place where he dwells. In Zion, God creates joy (v. 4) and sends help (v. 5).

Finally, in the third stanza (vv. 8-11), God provides refuge in the midst of violence. He enacts peace and destroys the weapons of war. Therefore, God's people can stop. They can stop struggling, stop worrying, and stop fighting to hold it all together and know that God, who is above the nations and the earth, is with his people as a refuge.

Preaching Pathways

1. **Confidence in uncertain times.** Despite our historical distance, we share the Psalmist's concerns. Natural disasters, political instability, war, and similar calamities fill our news cycles, and for many, the seeming inevitability of trouble induces immense anxiety. Psalm 46 redirects our attention to the God, who is present in and Lord over it all, and it encourages us to seek shelter in him rather than the alternatives.

2. **The nearness of God**. The psalm grounds our confidence in the proximity of God. God is not distant; he is present in this place and time. The language reminds us of the bookends in Matthew's gospel. In Matthew 1:23, the incarnate Jesus is named Emmanuel—"God with us." Then in Matthew 28:20, the risen Christ promises to be with us always to the end of the age. The psalm may also cue conversations about the immediacy of the Spirit and the mystery of

the Table.

Prayer from *Common Worship*

God of Jacob, when the earth shakes and the nations are in uproar, speak and let the storm be still; through Jesus Christ our Lord. Amen.

Psalm 51

A Prayer When You Have Failed

The psalm has three broad movements: *confession* (vv. 1-9), *renewal* (vv. 10-12), and *hope* (vv. 13-19). Though the historical tag links it to a time of personal sin and confession for King David, it is clear from the final verses that the psalm found use as a corporate confession in Israel's prayer life, leading it also to become one of most frequent "penitential psalms" prayed in the Church.

Movement 1: Confession.

This is the foundational movement for the psalm and the most textured. It is worth noting several things. *First, confession is rooted in a confidence in God's character.* God's "steadfast love" ("commitment" per Goldingay[1]) and "abundant mercy" are the reason the Psalmist can ask for God to be gracious. In fact, God's grace, steadfast love, and mercy are seen as YHWH's "canonical characteristics"—they are what Moses saw when he glimpsed at God's glory in Exodus 34:6.

Secondly, sin takes many forms. Though the confession appears to relate

---

1   Goldingay, *The Psalms*: Vol. 2, p. 126.

to a singular event, the language gives the indication that it is addressing sin throughout the course of one's life. Sin is described as *rebellion, waywardness*, and *failure*. Later in verses 3-6 sin is named again as *rebellion, failure,* and *waywardness*, but this time *evil* as added.

Thirdly, confession is a petition for God to remove the stain of sin. Goldingay notes[2] that the "effect of sin is comparable to the effect of contact with death," and that image appears later when the Psalmist prays to be washed with hyssop, a plant used to sprinkle water over a tent where someone has died in order to cleanse it. The structure of the first movement is a series of stepped lines. The verbs which bookend vv. 1-9, working from "outside in" of the lines of poetry, are *"wipe"* (v. 1 and v. 9), *"wash"* (v. 2a and v. 7b), *"purify"/"so that I may be pure"* (v. 2b and v. 7a), *"I acknowledge"/"make me acknowledge"* (v. 3 and v. 6), and *"I have failed"/"In failure"* (v. 4a and v. 5). This structure shows the emphasis on the desire for cleansing. But the structure also reveals what is at the heart of the prayer of confession by making one sentence the clear center of the poetic lines: a declaration of God's faithfulness ("You are faithful," v. 4b).

Movement 2: Renewal.

It is not enough to want the stain of sin removed; we need our inner being renewed. The word for "create" is the Hebrew word *"bara,"* which is used of God's work in Genesis. A fresh creative act is needed to return our lives to their created purpose: fidelity to God. The result is a consistent

---

2   Ibid.

and loyal spirit. Faithfulness to God requires an inner steadfastness that only God can provide.

Movement 3: Hope.

The Psalmist has hope that one day he will be able to "teach transgressors" God's ways and to be able to sing God's praise (vv. 13, 15). *The twofold sign of a new life is wisdom and worship.* Our interaction and relationship with others and with God have changed. This reminds us that sin is a failure on both planes—the horizontal and the vertical. The historical inscription on the psalm sets it in the context of David's sin against Uriah and his wife, yet David declares that his sin is against God alone (v. 4). This may be problematic, unless we take both together and accept the possibility that David's sin against humans was already evident, but the way in which his actions were also a sin against God needed to be drawn out and named; thus, the psalm focuses only on the vertical dimension of his sin. But the closing verses set the vertical alongside the horizontal, showing us that the fruit of repentance is evident in our relationships with both others and with God.

What is the reason for this hope? It is God himself. Words for "sin" are used 12 times in verses. 1-9, but only 2 times in verses 10-19. By contrast, "God" is named once in verses 1-9 and 6 times in verses 10-19. *"Sin gives way to God; with confession, sin gives way to God's presence."*[3]

---

3   Ibid., p. 140.

Preaching Pathways

1. **Confession is not begging God for mercy**. Confession is a response to the confidence in God's character as gracious, loving, and merciful. We do not confess our sins hoping that God will forgive us; we confess because we know that in Christ he already has.

2. **Sin leaves a stain, and it is a stain that has the stench of death.** Sin is always connected to death (remember Genesis 3?). Yet God and God alone can remove the stain of guilt. We can't self-talk our way out of it. We can't even remove it by "forgiving ourselves," important as that may be. We need someone from the outside to remove that stain.

3. **God wants to move from the *failure* to the *need*.** Our failure resulted in death. What we need now is a pure heart, to be made new, to be given a steadfast spirit. What was hoped for in the psalm is now received in Christ: God has put HIS Spirit in us, who renews our own spirits daily (cf. Romans 8).

4. **Sin affects our relationship with others and with God**. The fruit of repentance is wisdom in our relationship with others and worship toward God.

5. **God is our reason for hope!** Because God is gracious and merciful, we can confess our sins. Because God is faithful, we know he will make us new.

Prayer from *Common Worship*

Take away, good Lord, the sin that corrupts us; give us the sorrow that heals and the joy that praises and restore by grace your own image within us; that we may take our place among your people; in Jesus Christ our Lord. Amen.

Psalm 63

A Prayer for Desperate Times

At first glance this may appear like a lament psalm, especially because the opening verb for "seek" may lead one to the impression that the Psalmist is unable to reach God. But it is far more likely that the verb expresses an ongoing dynamic of the Psalmist's life with God.[1] In fact, all the verbs in the psalm are clues into what life with God is like: life with God involves "searching, thirsting, fainting, bringing to mind, muttering, cleaving."[2] So, this is a prayer of trust in desperate times. Moreover, it has every indication that the person praying is the king himself (possible narrative context is David in 2 Samuel 15-17). Power and wealth are not enough to insulate you from difficult times; in those moments, only a deep trust in the Lord will do.

The structure of the psalm loosely divides in thirds (vv. 1-4, vv. 5-8, v. 9-11), each of which deepens the sense of urgency. In the first stanza, the Psalmist declares his commitment to seek God—the verb here is vivid, implying a searching and waiting for daybreak (Luther translated this as "keep watch"). In the second stanza, the Psalmist recounts the faithfulness of the Lord to him in the past. The image of him lying on his bed calling to mind—even talking to himself—about how God has been his help is poignant. The result of remembrance is a commitment: just

---

1   Ibid., p. 255.

2   Ibid.

as God's loyal love is better than all that life can offer (v. 3), now the king vows to be "stuck" to God with a reciprocal fidelity[3]. The final stanza sets aside metaphor for a plainer description of his plight: there are enemies who want him dead. But he is confident that the king—now using the third person to refer not only to himself but to all who have come before and will come after—will find joy in God, the God who "stops up" the mouth of the lying, accusing, cursing enemy. There may be a Hebrew word-play here: the word for "seek" in verse 1 is *"sahar"* and the word for "stopped" in verse 9 is *"sakar"*; what begins with our seeking, ends with God stopping; our pursuit finds its fulfillment in God's putting an end to evil.

Preaching Pathways

1. **Power, wealth, and fame cannot insulate us from desperate situations.** It is a commonly held belief that if we just accumulate *more*, we will be able to insulate ourselves from hardship: health issues, enemies, betrayal, etc. This psalm repudiates that notion.

2. **Trust in God is not a hall pass from trials; it's the power to walk through them.** Jesus perhaps said it best: "In this world you will have trouble. But take heart! I have overcome the world" (John 16:33). It is the presence of our victorious Lord who helps us walk faithfully through trials.

---

3   Goldingay's translation of v. 8.

3. **Our ability to "stick with God" grows as we recount the faithfulness of God: how HE sticks with us** (vv. 3, 8). God's faithfulness to us is the ground and source of our own faithfulness to him.

4. **How do we "see God"?** Seeing God in the sanctuary has little to do with an existential experience of God's presence (there was nothing for a king to "see" in the sanctuary). Instead, this "sight" of God comes from the kind of prayer and worship that recounts who God is and what he has done. *To recall and rehearse and remember God's acts in the past is to see him again in the present.* (Think of the Lord's Table: a remembering that makes us "see," like the disciples on the road to Emmaus in Luke 24.)

5. **Our pursuit of God finds its satisfaction in God's putting the world to rights.** Life this side of resurrection requires ongoing trust because we won't see the final "stopping up" of evil yet. So we keep trusting because we know in the end it will happen.

Prayer from *Common Worship*

To you we come, radiant Lord, the goal of all our desiring, beyond all earthly beauty; gentle protector, strong deliverer, in the night you are our confidence; from first light be our joy; through Jesus Christ our Lord. Amen.

Psalm 84

A Psalm of the Lovely Dwelling Place

Written by the Sons of Korah, some of the great choral and orchestral leaders within Israel, this psalm is free of the perplexing interludes that characterize so many other songs. It's a holiday song, a song of unabated joy, a song to be sung at Israel's autumn festival, the Feast of Tabernacles. It's opening line—"How lovely is your dwelling place, Lord Almighty"—sets the tone. Stewart McCullough writes, "It is evident that the important thing about the temple, to our author, was that in and through the ritual, and perhaps despite it, *[men and women] somehow touched the garment of the living God"* (vv. 2, 7, 11-12)[1]. God is *available*. And the worshipper who continually gets in the presence of God is "blessed," is *happy*.

The importance of *place* is a recurring theme in this Psalm. Before Wendell Berry and Eugene Peterson, the Psalmist was telling us that *place matters*. In an age that has desacralized and denigrated the place of worship, the Psalmist says, "How lovely is your *dwelling place"* (v. 1). He goes on to discuss *"the courts of the Lord"* (v. 2) as a *"home"* (v. 3). And "even the sparrow" is wise enough to find *"a place* near your *altar"* (v. 3) in *"your house"* (v. 4). True worshippers journey to go "before God *in Zion"* (v. 7) and they exclaim "better is one day *in your courts*...in the

---

1   W. Stewart McCullough. *Interpreter's Bible Commentary* (Abingdon Press: 1955). Vol. 4, p. 452.

house of my God" (v. 10) than to dwell in the "tents of the wicked" (v. 10). "Blessed are those...who have set their hearts on pilgrimage" (v. 5). A highway is cut in the heart of the worshipper that causes her/him to get up and go to the house of the Lord to gather with the saints. In his *Introduction to Liturgical Theology*, Alexander Schmemann wrote: "The whole spirituality and liturgical piety of the early church could be summed up in the words of St. Ignatius of Antioch: 'Try to be together as much as possible.'"[2] There will always be something special about gathering with the people of God in the house of God. It is in his presence that we "go from strength to strength" (v. 7).

This psalm is also a reminder of what God will do with the shame of the worshipper. The "Valley of Baca" (*Bochim*, the "valley of weeping") was named after a particularly embarrassing episode in Israel's history (Judges 2:1-5). After the angel of the Lord rebuked them for breaking covenant, "the people lifted up their voices and wept" (Judges 2:4). I imagine that every time those worshippers passed through that valley they were reminded of "the sins of the fathers." But the Psalmist says that now, instead of the valley being filled with the tears of a wicked and adulterous people, the valley will be filled with the regenerating springs of God's autumn rains. The valley will now be nourished *from above* and no longer defined by the sins *committed below*. "As they pass through the Valley of Baca, they make it a place of springs" (v. 6). Grace, grace, grace.

---

2   St. Vladimir's Seminary Press: 1966. Page 141.

Preaching Pathways

1. **The preacher will be wise to remind the congregation of the importance of the gathered assembly of believers**. This is where we find life and meaning and hope.

2. **The preacher can take this opportunity to announce the Good News (Isaiah 61, Luke 4:18) that God knows what to do with our sin and shame**. He's the God who fills the "valley of tears" with showers of mercy and grace.

3. **This psalm reminds us that worship involves our entire *being***. It's an "all that is within us" thing (Psalm 103:1). "My *soul* yearns...my *heart* and *flesh* cry out to the living God" (v 2).

Prayer from *Common Worship*

Lord God, sustain us in this vale of tears with the vision of your grace and glory, that, strengthened by the bread of life, we may come to your eternal dwelling place; in the power of Jesus Christ our Lord. Amen.

Psalm 91

A Prayer in Peril

In Psalm 91, the writer confronts the perils of his world: disease, warfare, and beasts. If the Psalter's fourth book (90-106) relates to the Babylonian crisis, this psalm's initial audience may have been Judah's military, who particularly faced these threats during their deployment and who continually searched for protective strongholds, or, as per Goldingay,[1] Judah's king, who observed his troops from a distant tent (vv. 7-10). However, pestilence, violence, and wild animals are no respecters of persons; nor are hunter's snares (v. 3) or the things that go bump in the night (v. 5).

Though the Lord does not remove these clear and present dangers, he provides protection from and power over them. Those who trust in him, he will deliver and protect. Like a mother bird, he will cover his children with his wings; and like a military general, he will commission his angels to guard and ungird his people. The image of Yahweh as a bird may simply be a metaphor or it may point to the winged cherubim of the ark he dwells above. (See Exodus 19:4; Deuteronomy 32:11; Ruth 2:12; Psalm 5:11-12, 17:8, and 63:7 for additional occurrences.) The picture of God as the commander-in-chief of the heavenly hosts occurs throughout the Old Testament. Furthermore, the Lord will empower his people to tread

---

1   Goldingay, *Psalms*. Vol. 3, pp. 39-40.

and trample over the lion and the serpent. Therefore, God's people will not fear illness or enemies in the night or by day or in darkness or at the noonday. (Notice the alternation of time and light in verses 5 and 6.) After all, God will be with them in trouble, and he will reveal his salvation, which, in this case, indicates an immediate, bodily rescue.

Perhaps the most well-known portion of this psalm is verse 11. Matthew (4:6) and Luke (4:10-11) place these words on Satan's lips as he tempts Jesus to prove his divinity by throwing himself off of the Temple. Witherington notes that the Greek word for pinnacle (*pterugion*) is a variant of the Greek word for pinions (*pterugas*); therefore, the act of jumping may have represented a rejection of Yahweh's protection. Fascinatingly, he goes on to point out that the Psalmist declares victory over the serpent just two verses later. The New Testament echoes verse 13 in Jesus' crushing and yet still coming defeat of Satan (Romans 16:20) and his commissioning of the seventy (Luke 10:19).[2]

Preaching Pathways

1. **Trust in the Lord.** Psalm 91 implores us to trust God in an unsafe world. We typically rely on our abilities, our networks, and our resources to secure our present and future. Our hope usually abides in life's tangibles, in what we can assess, touch, or measure. But these things ultimately disappoint or disappear. Therefore, the

2   Ben Witherington, *Psalms Old and New: Exegesis, Intertextuality, and Hermeneutics* (Fortress Press, 2017), pp. 218-220.

Psalmist instructs us to let our hope dwell in the Most High and Almighty—in the intangible God who appears and delivers.

2. **Our imminent and ultimate rescue.** Texts that espouse the Lord's immediate help trouble us as much as, if not more than, they comfort us. The stories of devout believers who succumbed to cancer, godly men and women who died violently or unexpectedly, and loving parents who tragically lost their children are all too familiar to us. As a result, we question the veracity of the Psalmist's claims. Other psalms certainly give voice to our tension, while psalms like this one are meant to embolden our faith in the God who can rescue us now and will rescue us soon.

3. **Prayer as Conversation**. The first 13 verses of Psalm 91 alternate between second person ("you") and third person ("he") subjects, which suggests the psalm may have been read antiphonally in worship. But in the final verses, God personally speaks to us. The Psalms hold our words to God and his words to us. They teach us that the language of faith is always dialogical.

Prayer from *Common Worship*

Keep us, good Lord, under the shadow of your mercy and, as you have bound us to yourself in love, leave us not who call upon your name, but grant us salvation, made known in the cross of Jesus Christ our Lord. Amen.

Psalm 103

Bless God Who Makes My Life Right!

Psalm 103 is as towering and memorable an anthem of praise as one is likely to find in the Psalter. *"Praise the Lord, my soul; all my inmost being praise his holy name!"* exclaims the Psalmist in verse 1. And why should God be praised? The answer is clear and obvious: for "all of his benefits" (v.2). God is not praised in some sterile theological void, nor is he blessed for being a cogent ideological construct. Not for this worshiper, anyway. God is praised because he is the One who has made and continues to make life go right. *"...who forgives all your sins, and heals all your diseases, who redeems your life from the pit and crowns you with love and compassion, who satisfies your desires with good things so that your youth is renewed like the eagle's"* (vv. 3-5). When life works the way it is supposed to, we find ourselves continually reborn in vitality and strength. Yahweh is the giver of that gift. Jesus put the matter tersely: "The thief comes only to steal and kill and destroy; I have come that they may have life and have it to the full" (John 10:10).

But what does "life's going right" hinge on? What is it contingent upon? The merits of the worshiper? Not by a long shot. For the author of Psalm 103, everything is dependent upon the kindness of God who is not treating us "as our sins deserve" or repaying us "according to our iniquities" (v. 10). He is the "compassionate and gracious" God, "slow to anger, abounding in love" (v. 8). Were the full consequence of our misdeeds visited upon us, we wouldn't survive. We'd find ourselves swallowed up in the chaos of our own making. Said the Psalmist in Psalm 130:3, "If you, Yahweh, kept a record of sins, Lord, who could stand?" Indeed. And it turns that Yahweh's will to forgive, to make life right again, outpaces our penchant for failure: "As far as the east is from the west, so far has he removed our transgressions from us" (Ps 103:12). *Yahweh's steady determination to do his people good beyond their deserving is the bedrock and only hope for life's ongoing wholesomeness.* Seen this way, Psalm 103 is an anthem to the gospel of God's grace.

Preaching Pathways

1. **"Forget not all his benefits..."** According to Paul, when the first humans defected from their Creator, a door was opened, and Death came riding into the human experience. The entirety of God's redemptive work is to push back and finally overcome the disordering of human life that comes about by sin. We taste it in part here. We will taste it in full when Christ returns. This psalm is a powerful reminder of God's will to make life work the way it was intended to work.

2. **Grace is the bedrock**. Life's working the way it ought to be is never a human achievement (though it does require our participation). It is God's limitless kindness to human beings with whom he is in covenant relationship that makes life work right. Grace, lived in and celebrated, is the bedrock of wholesomeness.

3. **Worship is the result.** When the concrete goodness of God comes spilling into our lives and we recognize it as such, the result is an anthem of praise. We bless the Lord, having remembered all his benefits.

Prayer from *Common Worship*

Merciful Lord, as we come from dust and return to dust, show us the face of our Redeemer, that in our frailty we may bless your name and praise you all our days; through Jesus Christ our Lord. Amen.

54

Psalm 112

A Psalm of the *Good* Kind of Retribution

Psalm 112 is classified as a "song of retribution," which we typically think of in terms of God "getting back at" the disloyal and disobedient. We immediately think *punishment*. We imagine *judgment*. But retribution is a sword that cuts both ways, which is to say that God is also the God who honors and exalts and "pays back" according to one's righteousness. "Righteousness" in this psalm denotes a life of integration and wholeness. Someone who lays her head on the pillow at night with a clear conscience, having honored Yahweh the best she can and having repented of her missteps at the moment she recognized them. It's also important to remember that "righteousness" in Psalm 112 is *not* about one's *essence* or *ethos*, but about one's *actions*. The life of faith is a life of *obedience*, of keeping Torah. Remember Jesus' words: "If you love me, you will obey my commands" (John 14:15). In a world that wants to spiritualize everything, this psalm reminds us that *what we do matters*.

There is a simple moral calculus in this psalm—"Good will come to him who is generous and lends freely, who conducts his affairs with justice" (v. 5). When you cooperate with God, your "children will be mighty in the land" (v.2), and "wealth and riches are in [your] house" (v. 3). The overarching tone is a tone of *happiness* for the one who keeps Torah (vv. 1b-9). Essentially, this psalm wants us to know that the covenanting God—and the world he made—is reliable, and that "in the end he/she [the righteous one] will look in triumph on his/her foes" (v. 8).

Many will read Psalm 112 and immediately cry foul, citing the tribulations of the world in which we live. *Don't you see what's going on out there?* It will help the reader to understand where Psalm 112 "fits" in the canonical puzzle. Not every *text* can do *everything*. In a lecture I once attended through Fuller Seminary, Dr. John Goldingay noted:

There are theologians and philosophers who are good at raising questions, and others who are good at providing answers. Proverbs belongs more in the second category, Job and Ecclesiastes more in the first. David Hubbard, former President of the seminary where I teach, put it this way: "Proverbs says, 'These are the rules for life. Try them and you will find that they work.' Job and Ecclesiastes say, 'We did, and they don't.' Proverbs offers us ground rules for understanding life. Job and Ecclesiastes help us to live with experiences that belie the ground rules.

We'll let Ecclesiastes and Job and the psalms of disorientation be what they are meant to be in the canon. But we must also let Psalm 112 be what it was meant to be—an affirmation that the righteous God blesses his righteous ones: "Blessed is the one who fears the Lord" (v. 1). When it's all said and done, and when Yahweh comes to balance the ledger, it will end up working out beautifully for the righteous.

Preaching Pathways

1. **The preacher will be wise to take the opportunity to remind the hearer that obedience matters and always has for the people of God**. The sloppy "don't judge me," "live and let live" culture in which we live wants to move the ancient boundary stones, but God's people hear the call to "keep" these commandments (Deut. 11:18; Prov. 7:3; John 14:14, 21).

2. **The preacher will be wise to help people understand where Psalm 112 fits in the sweep of Scripture**. It is not a denial of evil. It would not seek to diminish the grief in which the suffering saint lives. But, like Aaron and Hur holding up a collapsing Moses (Exodus 17:11), Psalm 112 can serve as a support to the one who suffers. "In the end, you will look in triumph on your foes" (v. 8).

Prayer from *Common Worship*

Generous God, save us from the meanness that calculates its interest and hoards its earthly gain; as we have freely received, so may we freely give; in the grace of Jesus Christ our Lord. Amen.

Psalm 119

A Prayer for Guidance

Psalm 119 is a literary feat. It is made up of 176 verses, by far the collection's longest poem, divided into 22 sets of eight lines. The sets form what is known as an "alphabetic acrostic." Each set corresponds to a consecutive letter in the Hebrew alphabet with each line in the set beginning with that letter. So, in the first set, each of the eight verses starts with a word that begins with *aleph*, the first letter in the Hebrew alphabet. The pattern continues with each subsequent set. (Psalms 25, 111, 112, 145 and Lamentations 3 are also acrostics.)

The psalm's composer may have chosen to pen eight verses for each letter to match the eight synonyms he uses for the Law: law (*torah*), decrees (*edut*), precepts (*piqqudim*), statutes (*huqqim*), commandments (*mitzvot*), ordinances (*mishpatim*), word/words (*davar/devarim*), and saying/sayings (*imrah/amarot*). Lead by torah, each of these words occurs twenty or more times in the psalm. Because of its emphasis on the Law, Psalm 119 may be classified as a Torah Psalm alongside of Psalm 1 and Psalm 19. Like Psalm 1, Psalm 119 anchors the blessed life in the observance of the Law.

Psalm 119 belongs to the fifth book in the Psalter (107-150), which is frequently associated with Judah's return from exile. Though we cannot definitively tie its composition to this time period, we know that the Torah took on greater significance during Israel's captivity. Without a temple to offer sacrifices, God's people accentuated ethical obedience. This stress continued in the Second Temple Period. Interestingly, the Psalmist even asks the Lord to accept these meditations on the Law as freewill offerings (119:108).

Psalm 119 primarily addresses Yahweh devotionally. The Psalmist praises the Lord for the Law, petitions God for direction, and commits himself to knowing and keeping God's guiding words. Throughout his work, he expresses a deep affection for the Torah. He treasures, rejoices, delights, and even loves God's Law for it is right and good, reliable and true; and through it, God grants life and strength, wisdom and freedom, comfort and stability in all circumstances to those who walk in its light.

Preaching Pathways

1. **The Law as grace**. The Psalmist's affection for the Torah may startle those who view the Law negatively. On account of a misunderstanding of certain New Testament passages, many characterize the Old Testament as a library of law and the New Testament as a library of grace. But the two testaments contain both, and they consider the Law a grace. Psalm 119 reminds us that God gave his Law to the people he set free so that they might learn to live free lives. When we proved unable to follow God's ways, God sent Jesus to fulfill the Law for us and the Spirit to fulfill the Law in us.

2. **Practices for reading Scripture**. Psalm 119 calls us to devote ourselves to Scriptures and introduces several practices for reading the Bible, including memorization and meditation. It also includes several humble requests for understanding (e.g., 18, 27, 34), which highlight the essential relationship between study and prayer. As Christians, we read prayerfully and pray Scripturally so that our hearts might be transformed, along with our minds, and our longings and pleas might be channeled and directed by God's revealed will for our lives.

3. **Obedience**. For the Psalmist, doing is the "telos," the end result, of knowing God's Word (see Matthew 7:24-27). He seeks to conform his life to the Torah as an expression of his adoration and fidelity to Yahweh and not out of a legalistic obligation or a fear of damnation. Though he fully realizes the benefits of obedience and the consequences of defiance, he is relationally motivated. Yahweh is his God and he is Yahweh's servant.

Prayer from *Common Worship*

God of mercy, swift to help us, as our lips pour forth your praise, fill our hearts with the peace you give to those who wait for your salvation in Jesus Christ our Lord. Amen.

Psalm 121

A Psalm of the Talkative Saints

Pilgrims on their way to worship in Jerusalem were traveling through rugged conditions. The arid desert struck fear deep in the heart of every wayfarer. Then add to that the existence of armed robbers who knew it was the season of pilgrimage to Jerusalem. For them, this would be like shooting fish in a barrel. "With this much traffic, surely we'll be able to pick off someone!" It is easy to imagine the pilgrims thinking to themselves, "Maybe *this* is going to be the moment when everything falls apart?"

The defenseless worshippers paid to sleep in guarded encampments with sentries of guards perched on the surrounding hills. The hope was that the guards would be able to stave off any terrorist activity for the night. So, as he crawled into his tent that night, the God-fearing Jew looked up to the hills and wondered if the guards would be able to do their job. "I lift my eyes to the hills. Where does my help come from?" (v. 1). The Psalmist gives assurance—"He will not let your foot slip. He who watches over you will not slumber" (v. 3).

The literary format of this psalm is of some interest. It's an antiphonal call-and-response psalm. So it might go something like this:

The Psalmist's Question: *"I lift my eyes to the hills. Where does my help* *come from?"*

The Community Response: *"Your help comes from the Lord, the maker of heaven and earth!"*

Back and forth they call and respond, bolstering each other's faith along the journey to the house of God. This psalm reminds us that the collective faith of the family of God undergirds the failing believer. "You're going to make it," we remind each other. And the payoff erupts on the hearer: When you get tired and when the saints around you get tired, when all of you are helpless to watch over your situation, "He who watches over Israel will neither slumber nor sleep" (v. 4).

These people lived in a pre-scientific world and were therefore very superstitious. Watching travelers collapse day after day, they naturally feared sunstroke. There was no shade. To that the Psalmist says, "The Lord is your keeper; the Lord is *the shade at your right hand"* (v. 5). As strong as the elements are, the Lord our God is stronger. The people felt threatened by demonic attack. "The popular mind...assumed that a demon in the sun or the moon was the agent of the evil".[1] But the Psalmist brings comfort: "The *sun* will not harm you by day, nor the *moon* by night. *The Lord will keep you from all evil"* (vv. 6-7). This reminds one of what Proverbs 26:2 says: "Like a fluttering sparrow or a darting swallow, an undeserved curse does not come to rest." God will keep you. You're not on your own. "No evil shall befall you, nor any plague come near your dwelling place" (Ps 91:10).

---

1   McCullough, *IBC*. Page 647.

Preaching Pathways

1. **The preacher will find a great opportunity to highlight the call-and-response format**, and to emphasize the way the collective faith of the family of God undergirds the failing believer. This is a great opportunity to speak to people who find themselves weak and need someone to speak strength into their hearts.

2. **This is a great psalm to dramatize**. Paint a picture for the congregation. Help them imagine themselves in a scary, enemy-infested wilderness. Help them imagine journeying through the hot desert where there is no water. Maybe consider bringing a tent on stage to help them envision crawling into their tent and staring out to see the guards on the distant hills. Maybe consider bringing some water up on the stage with you for the climactic moment of the sermon to demonstrate how God provides for us, satisfies our need against all odds. This one could be fun!

Prayer from *Common Worship*

Lord, ever watchful and faithful, we look to you to be our defense and we lift our hearts to know your help; through Jesus Christ our Lord. Amen.

Psalm 139

A Prayer to the God Who Knows Me Completely

Every Christian should have Psalm 139 committed to memory. It is perhaps the finest and most poetic statement of God's intimate knowledge of and care for each and every human being found in the Scriptures. Robert Alter comments on the opening lines of verse 1 *("You have searched me, Yahweh, and you know me.")* saying that "These words inaugurate one of the most remarkably introspective psalms in the canonical collection...this poem is essentially a meditation on God's searching knowledge of man's innermost thoughts, on the limitations of human knowledge, and on God's inescapable presence throughout the created world."[1] The Psalmist affirms that God knows him inside and out, that even if he exhausted himself in the effort, he would never be able to escape God's *ruach* (breath, Spirit) or his *panim* (face, Presence), that God had marked out his days ahead of time and formed him in his mother's womb, and that even now, no matter what he did, God's hand was upon him like a potter shaping him for untold beauty, purpose, and meaning.[2]

Realizing this awakens wonder and awe in the Psalmist. *"How precious*

---

1 Robert Alter, *The Book of the Psalms: A Translation with Commentary* (W. W. Norton and Company, 2007), p. 479.

2 Ibid., p. 480. Alter's comment on verse 5: "'You set your palm upon me' is not a menacing act but the gesture of the potter."

to me are your thoughts, God! How vast is the sum of them!" (v. 17).
His meditation on God's everywhere-presence and intimate knowledge
of his life staggers him. "When I awake, I am still with you." (v. 18b).
Alter comments on verse 18 saying: "What the poet may be imagining
is that after the long futile effort of attempting to count God's infinite
thoughts, he drifts off into exhaustion, then awakes to discover that
God's eternal presence, with all those endless divine thoughts, is still with
him."[3] He falls asleep thinking of God and awakes with God's presence
still lingering in the air. The feeling generates even deeper devotion—a
devotion that is consistent with the poem's entire claim: "Search me, God,
and know my heart" (v. 23). Knowing that his ways are already totally
transparent to God, he seeks to live transparently before God. So living,
the Potter will shape him for everlasting life (v. 24).

Preaching Pathways

1. **God's intimate knowledge of human beings.** He knows us inside
    and out. Nothing is secret. Nothing is hidden. And because we know
    that his intentions are good, we can trust him with this intimate
    knowledge. Real life is found in living transparently before the One
    who already knows us better than we know ourselves.

2. **God's relentless pursuit of us**. Is God with us in our light? Of course.
    But even more profound is this poem's declaration that God is with

---

3   Ibid., p. 482.

us even in our darkness. To that extent, it lays out the gospel of Jesus powerfully ahead of time. Jesus is God of very God sent into the "far country" of our darkness and isolation to find us and bring us home. The Psalmist's words, therefore, were truer than he realized. The God he worshiped is the Father of Jesus, who willingly plunged himself into our darkness.

Prayer from *Common Worship*

Creator God, may every breath we take be for your glory, may every footstep show you as our way that, trusting in your presence in this world, we may, beyond this life, still be with you where you are alive and reign for ever and ever. Amen.

Psalm 150

A Final Hallelujah

It's helpful to know where you're going. Any journey is *bearable* if we know the destination is *desirable*. On the road of life, we sometimes wonder, *"How is this all going to end up? Will things ever be made right? Will the broken be put back together? Will justice come about? Will lament turn to praise?"*

I have a friend who likes to say that Psalm 1 is the Torah restated and what follows is all the "drama" of life; then Psalm 150 is the final "Hallelujah." Torah—Drama—Hallelujah. This may be a helpful way of characterizing the order of the Psalter. Psalm 1 is a re-articulation of the blessedness of the way of obedient faithfulness, but then the drama of life unfolds through the next 148 psalms, revealing the ups and downs of the life of faith. Through it all the Psalmist *keeps talking to God*, keeps trusting *that God is listening* and that *God cares*. And so, finally, in the end she erupts in praise! God has been faithful *through it all!* She wants God to be praised *in every place* and *with every instrument. The great hymnbook of Israel does not end in a minor key.*

It is Psalm 150 that shows that Psalm 1 was right after all: "The Lord knows the way of the righteous." God is intimately acquainted with every bend in the road, every slide downhill, every climb uphill, every mountain, every valley. He *knows* us and the journey we've been on. And God himself will see to it—indeed through Christ has already made it so—that the end will be praise. Sorrow will not win; Death will not have the last word; the Enemy does not laugh last. He who sits in Heaven laughs. And all who belong to God will shout with praise. In fact, the ending is *so* good that it isn't just good in our eyes; it is good before *all creation. Let everything that has breath say a final Hallelujah!*

This joy rightly culminates in praise. C. S. Lewis, in his *Reflection on the Psalms*, wrote, "I think we delight to praise what we enjoy because the praise not merely expresses but completes the enjoyment; it is its appointed consummation."[1] In other words, *praise is the completion of joy.* For the Christian, praise can even be the *anticipation of joy in the end.* We don't need to wait until the end, until the restoration of all things, to sing "Hallelujah"; we can begin singing it now, even as the Psalmist did.

Preaching Pathways

1. **Do you ever think about where this life with God is heading?**
   Sometimes we get so fixated on the *immediate* that we forget about the *ultimate.* We can get so frustrated with God for the way things are working out right now that we forget the song does not end in a minor key. Even if we can't find a song now, it can be important to believe that *one day* we *will* sing.

---

1   Harvest Book/Harcourt, Inc.: 1958, p. 95.

2. **What would it look like to sing a "Hallelujah" now in advance?** If Christians really are for whom the "age to come" has already dawned, then we are living in the "Hallelujah" even now. What would it look like to sing songs of the morning while living at midnight? This is what Paul and Silas did in prison. And this is what we can do each time we gather as the Church.

3. **Praise is the *completion* and the *anticipation* of joy.** How might we begin singing now as a result of the hints of God's faithfulness already on display in our lives? These "stabs of joy," as C. S. Lewis called them, remind us of what's coming. Let every joy—every small and every great joy—overflow in praise today.

Prayer from *Common Worship*

God of life and love, whose Son was victorious over sin and death, make us alive with his life, that the whole world may resound with your praise; through Jesus Christ our Lord. Amen.

Recommended Resources

Commentaries

Robert Alter. *The Book of the Psalms: A Translation with Commentary*. W. W. Norton and Company: New York, 2007. (Alter is a non-Christian Jew who is steeped in the language and thought of the Psalms. His translations and perspectives on words and phrases are invaluable. The Christian reader won't always agree with Alter's non-Christian perspective, but he will be enriched.)

John Goldingay. *Psalms*. 3 vols. Baker Commentary on the Old Testament. Baker Academic: Grand Rapids, 2008. (Very thorough commentary that gives analysis, interpretation, and theological implications for each psalm. Good introduction as well.)

Derek Kidner. *Psalms*. 2 vols. Tyndale Old Testament Commentary Series. InterVarsity Press: Downers Grove, 2008. (Another good commentary with a nice introduction. Readable and easy-to-access handling of each psalm.)

Other Resources

(Psalms-specific)

Walter Brueggemann. *The Message of the Psalms*. Fortress Press: Minneapolis, 1985.

C. S. Lewis. *Reflections on the Psalms*. HBC Publishers: New York, 1958.

Tremper Longman, III. *How to Read the Psalms*. InterVarsity Press: Downers Grove, 1980.

Claus Westerman. *The Psalms: Structure, Content, and Message*. Augsburg: Minneapolis, 1980.

Ben Witherington. *Psalms Old and New: Exegesis, Intertextuality, and Hermeneutics* Fortress Press: Minneapolis, 2017.

N. T. Wright. *The Case for the Psalms*. HarperCollins: New York, 2013.

(Works with chapters or sections dealing with the Psalms)

Hans Boersma. *Scripture as Real Presence*. Baker: Grand Rapids, 2017. (For the more academically minded, Chapter 6 of this book deals with how the ancients understood the spiritual and moral value of music and the way in which the earliest Christian interpreters took up that understanding and weaved it into their Christological reading of the Psalms. Groundbreaking and highly thought-provoking work.)

Dietrich Bonhoeffer. *Life Together*. HarperCollins: New York, 1954. (On pages 44-50 of this book, Bonhoeffer gives a brilliant, simple exposition of the "Christological ground" of the Psalter. It will forever alter how you read the Psalms.)

Gordon Fee and Douglas Stewart. *How to Read the Bible for All Its Worth*. Zondervan: Grand Rapids, 1993. (Chapter 11 deals specifically with understanding and interpreting the Psalms. Very good and highly recommended reading.)

Eugene Peterson. *Working the Angles*. Eerdmans: Grand Rapids, 1987. (Chapter 1 of this book provides a really nice summary of how important the Psalms were in formation of the ancient Hebrew's self-understanding. Highly recommended reading for understanding the Psalms as formation.)

Made in the USA
Middletown, DE
06 February 2019